Everyone WRITE

Book 1
Grades 1–2

by Linda Ward Beech

SNIFFEN COURT BOOKS/NEW YORK

Artists:

Felicia Bond, 20, 24, 26, 36, 48, 57
Maxie Chambliss, 7, 8, 9, 10, 11, 12, 13, 14, 15, 18, 30, 31, 32, 33, 34, 35, 40, 44, 46, 47, 50, 53, 54, 55, 59, 61
Ellen Matlach, 16, 17, 19, 21, 22, 23, 25, 29, 38, 39, 42, 43, 45, 51, 52, 58, 60, 62, 63, 64
Manuel Rivera, 28

Cover Artist:

Susan Swan

ISBN 0-930790-02-2

Copyright © 1988 by Sniffen Court Books, a division of Design Counsel, Inc., 153 East 30th Street, New York, New York 10016. Permission is granted to reproduce the copy masters in this book in complete pages, with the copyright notice, for instructional use and not for resale.

Printed in the United States of America

Table of Contents

To the Teacher — 5

Who Is Jim? — 7
Making Inferences

The Hidden Kite — 8
Using Logic

The Lost Note — 9
Solving a Problem

Where Are They? — 10
Perceptual Organization

The "B" Mystery — 11
Predicting Outcomes

What Next? — 12
Predicting Outcomes

Phone Fun — 13
Drawing Conclusions

Make an Animal — 14
Identifying Relationships

Whhoo-o-o Is There? — 15
Drawing Conclusions

The Missing Food — 16
Part/Whole Relationships

Together We Go — 17
Classifying

Opposite Annie — 18
Anticipating Probabilities

Rainy Day — 19
Making References

Lost and Found — 20
Using Logic

Pack Up — 21
Making Inferences

Riddle Faces — 22
Part/Whole Relationships

Silly Signs — 23
Classifying

Sand Castles — 24
Anticipating Probabilities

A-maze-ing Trip — 25
Sequencing

Haunted House — 26
Classifying

Haunted House — 27
Synthesizing

A Time Piece — 28
Part/Whole Relationships

What Happened? — 29
Developing Story Logic

The Green Cat Paws — 30
Making Inferences

The Green Cat Paws — 31
Predicting Outcomes

Who Is Ed? — 32
Making Inferences

Put Out the Fire — 33
Solving a Problem

Riding High — 34
Solving a Problem

In the Mud — 35
Solving a Problem

From Clue to Clue — 36
Sequencing

From Clue to Clue — 37
Developing Story Logic

The Empty Cage — 38
Building Hypotheses

Name the Place — 39
Proposing Alternatives

Just Pretend — 40
Real and Make-Believe

Just Pretend *Real and Make-Believe*	41	**The Silly Dream** *Building Hypotheses*	53
Finding the Words *Recognizing Structure*	42	**Cartoon Capers** *Making Inferences*	54
Can Code *Recognizing Structure*	43	**Cartoon Capers** *Predicting Outcomes*	55
Mirror Mary *Anticipating Probabilities*	44	**Title Time** *Summarizing*	56
Birthday Notes *Conducting a Project*	45	**Over the Hill** *Building Hypotheses*	57
What's the Problem? *Identifying Problems*	46	**Valentine Message** *Conducting a Project*	58
Talk Time *Drawing Conclusions*	47	**Story in a Picture** *Judging Relevance*	59
Island Hop *Classifying*	48	**How Come?** *Proposing Alternatives*	60
Island Hop *Synthesizing*	49	**Now What?** *Predicting Outcomes*	61
Help Wanted *Using Sequence*	50	**Partners and Pairs** *Comparing and Contrasting*	62
V's Wheels *Developing Story Logic*	51	**Opening Doors** *Part/Whole Relationships*	63
In the Bag *Building Hypotheses*	52	**A-maze-ing Ride** *Sequencing*	64

To the Teacher

The reproducible pages of this book will help students hone the skills they need for writing. Most importantly, each page focuses students on the thinking processes required of a writer. Students are guided in writing creatively, logically, and intelligently. As students master the thinking skills inherent in the writing process, they develop a sense of independence and confidence as writers.

You can use these pages both in and out of the classroom. They can be assigned as deskwork or homework. They can also become the core of a classroom writing center. You will find pages that are relevant to curriculum areas such as science, social studies, and language arts. You will find pages that relate to popular holidays. A variety of original writing activities ensures continuing interest and growth for your young writers.

Tips for Use

Book 1 includes a number of cut and paste and coloring activities so you will want to have the appropriate materials on hand.

For beginning writers, it may be more comfortable to tell their stories orally rather than write them down. You may also take dictation from these students. Many will have far more to say than they can actually write, and you won't want the physical act of writing to interfere with the flow of fresh ideas. If possible, utilize teacher's aides, older students, or parents to assist in dictation.

For students who are writing their own stories down, you will want to have additional paper on hand for pieces that run long.

Most pages are designed to be open-ended. Encourage students to try out unusual approaches and solutions. Some suggested guidelines for answers appear at the end of this section.

Ideas for Presentation

Many pages lend themselves to lively discussion. You will want to take advantage of such learning opportunities once the writing activities have been completed.

Students can make booklets of their own writing as they complete pieces during the school year.

In some instances you may want to make class booklets of students' work for a particular page.

Use the students' finished pages as the central point of a bulletin board display.

To promote an understanding of audience, have students read their finished work to other classes or to parents.

Many pages call for original artwork as well as creative writing. Such pages can become the focus of a class art show.

Guidelines for Answers

page 8
Most students will suggest that Jim can see and reach the Kite, but accept any reasonable solution.

page 9
Most students will suggest that Jim can lean over the stream and get the note, but accept any reasonable solution.

page 17
bed/hammock; beach umbrella/rain umbrella; street lamp/flashlight; bench/chair; fire/stove

page 21
Students should recognize that the winter items (ear muffs, long underwear, scarf, mittens) would not be needed on most summer vacations. However, logical exceptions are acceptable.

page 24
Students should understand that the tide will probably wash away the sand castle and move the shells and boat. People may possibly come to the beach and make other changes.

page 27
WHO: ghost, skelton, cat; WHERE: attic, stairs, bedroom

page 29
Things that stayed the same: cone, hammer, pad, ruler. Things that changed: ice cream, butter, and candle all melted. Some students may note that the metal part of the hammer would become very hot.

page 33
Most students will suggest that the elephant will put the fire out, but any reasonable solutions are acceptable.

page 34
Most students will suggest that the elephant can lift Ned up, but any reasonable solutions are acceptable.

page 35
Most students will suggest that the elephant can push or pull the car, but any reasonable solutions are acceptable.

page 42
For example: at, cat, bat, lab, tab, race, ace, brace, lace, rate, late, let, bet, tear, ear, bear, are, car, bare, crate, tale, reel

page 49
ANIMALS: whale, gull, crab; PEOPLE: diver, swimmer, sailor

page 50
Student's directions should account for the fact that Sally has two different socks and Kirk is under his cot.

page 62
horn/trumpet; canoe/ship; football/baseball; pitchfork/fork; clock/watch

Name _____

Who Is Jim?

Cut and paste the correct pictures to finish the story.

Jim is tall.

Jim is a ☐

He has ☐ .

Jim has 4 long ☐ .

His head is on a big long ☐ .

Draw Jim in the box.
Tell one more thing about him.

Jim

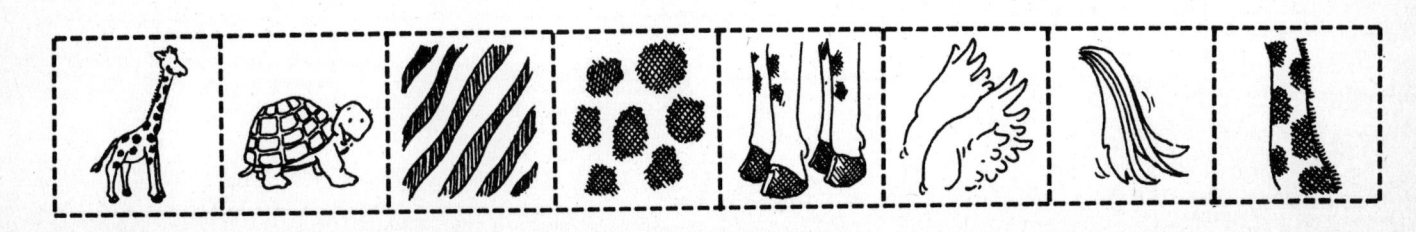

_____

_____

Making Inferences — 7 — Everyone WRITE

Name _____

The Hidden Kite

The kite got away.
Pat can't find it.
How does Jim find it?

Draw a picture.
Write the story.

Using Logic — 8 — Everyone WRITE

Name _____

The Lost Note

Jim lost the note.
It is on the other side.
How can Jim get the note?

Draw a picture.
Write the story.

Solving a Problem — 9 — Everyone WRITE

Name _____

Where Are They?

Mac and Jim are lost.
Look for the J's to find Jim.
Color these parts brown and white.

Look for the M's to find Mac.
Color the M parts green.

What does Mac say when he sees Jim?
What does Jim say?
Write their words in the spaces.

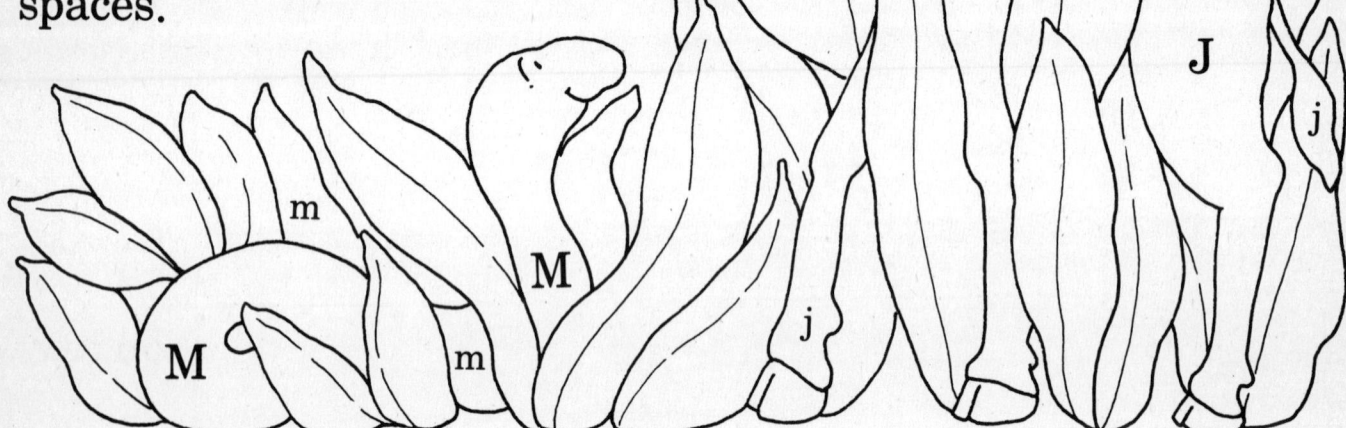

_____
_____
_____
_____

Perceptual Organization | 10 | Everyone WRITE

Name _____

The "B" Mystery

Finish the story about the 🐝 .

Use your own pictures.

This is Buzz 🐝 . He goes from 🌸 2 🌸 .

He makes 🍯 🪮🪮 in his 🐝hive .

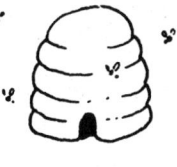

But 1 day 🐝 🪚 that some 🍯 was missing. Who 8 it?

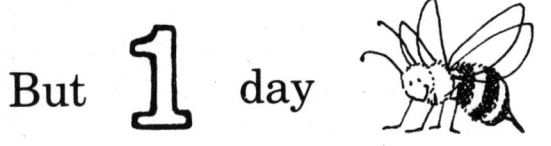

It was [____] ! She put [____] on her [____] . Then she [____] it.

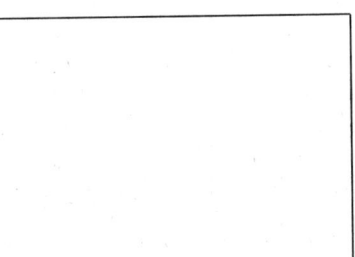

Predicting Outcomes — 11 — Everyone WRITE

Name _____

What Next?

What might happen next in the story?

Draw a picture to show.

Write about your ending.

Predicting Outcomes — 12 — Everyone WRITE

Copyright © 1988 Sniffen Court Books

Name _____

Phone Fun

Write what the man says.

_____

_____

Write what the lady says.

_____

_____

Drawing Conclusions — 13 — Everyone WRITE

Name _____

Make an Animal

Draw a make-believe animal.
Tell about your animal.
What does it do?
What does it eat?
What is its name?

_____
_____
_____
_____
_____
_____
_____

Identifying Relationships

Name _____

Whhoo-o-o Is There?

Who is hiding in Tom's house?
Follow the dots to find out.
What does he say?
Write it in the space.

_____

_____

What does Tom say?
Write it in the space.

_____

Drawing Conclusions   15   Everyone WRITE

Name _____

The Missing Food

Who ate some of Tom's food?
Part of it is gone!
Finish drawing all the food.
Then cut and paste the
pictures to use in the story.

Tom was mad! Part of his [   ] was gone. So was some [   ]. Who took some of his [   ] and [   ]? And where was the rest of his [   ]?

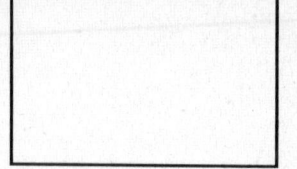

Write an ending to tell who did it.

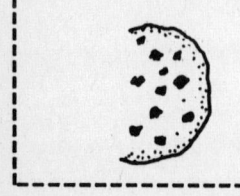

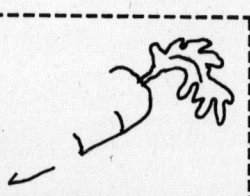

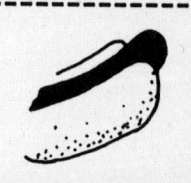

_____

_____

Part/Whole Relationships   16   Everyone WRITE

Copyright © 1988 Sniffen Court Books

Name _____

Together We Go

Find something in the top row and something in the bottom row that are used for the same thing.

Draw a line to match each pair.

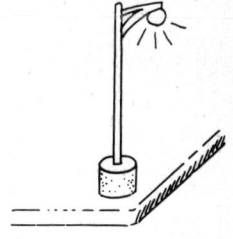

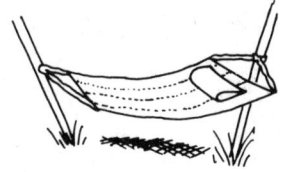

Choose one pair.
Write how they are alike.

_____
_____
_____
_____
_____

Classifying — 17 — Everyone WRITE

Name _____

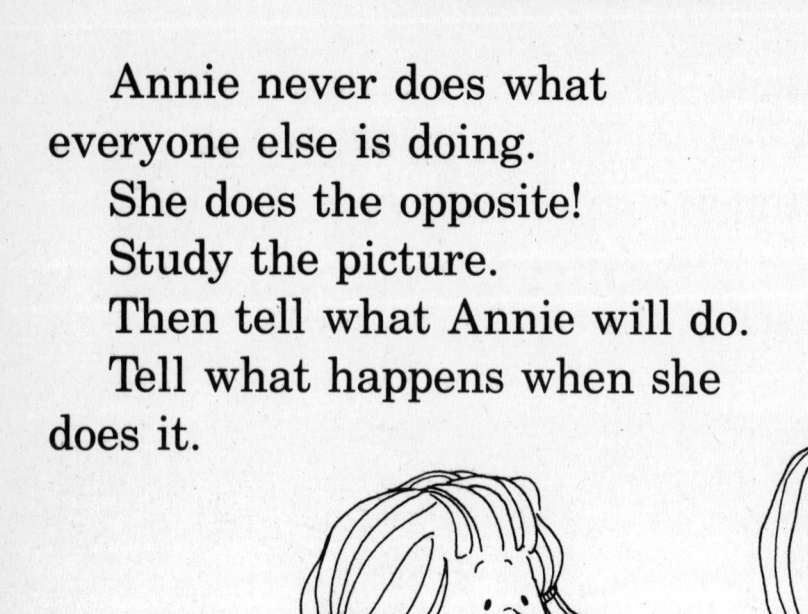

Opposite Annie

Annie never does what everyone else is doing.
She does the opposite!
Study the picture.
Then tell what Annie will do.
Tell what happens when she does it.

_____
_____
_____
_____
_____

Anticipating Probabilities — **Everyone WRITE**

Name _____

Rainy Day

It's a rainy day and you can't go out.

Which things can you play with?

Draw a line from the toy chest to each one.

Write a story about your rainy day.

_____
_____
_____
_____
_____

Making References · 19 · Everyone WRITE

Name _____

Lost and Found

These things are in the Lost and Found.

Cut and paste the picture to show what goes inside each box or case.

Pick one box.
Tell who lost it.
Where?
How?

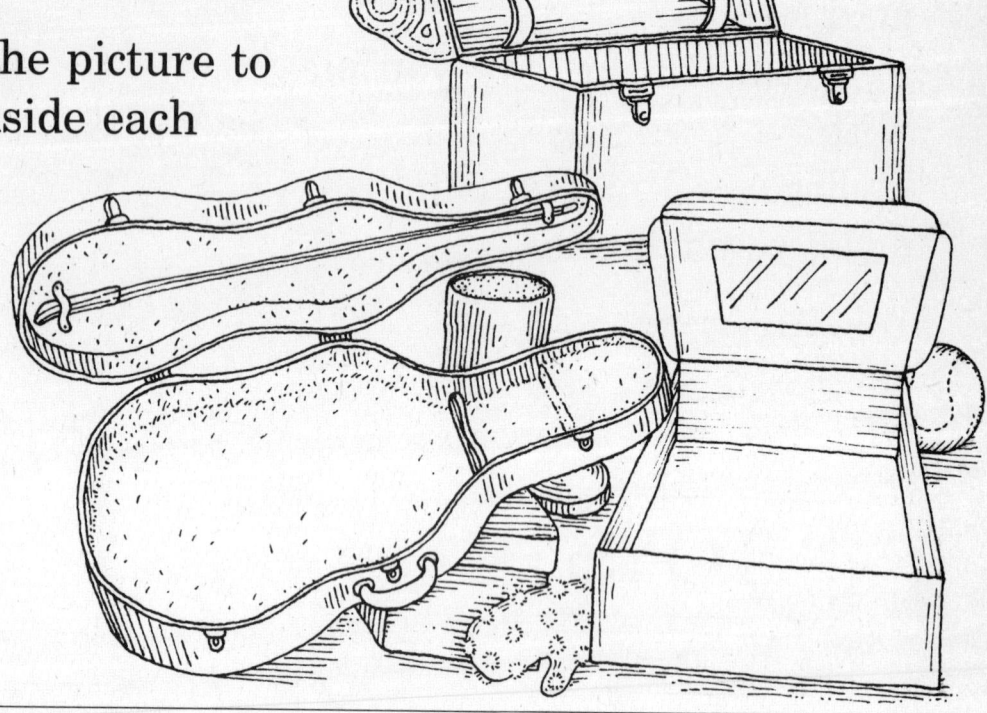

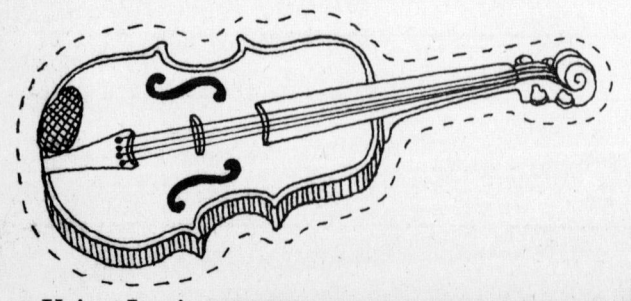

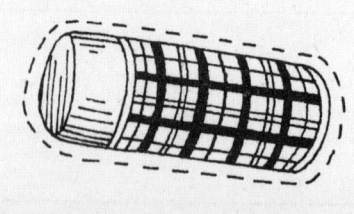

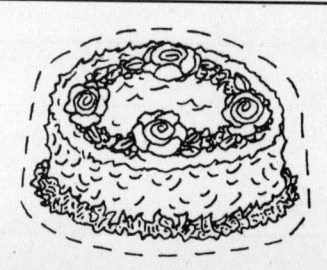

_____
_____
_____
_____
_____

Using Logic　　20　　Everyone WRITE

Name _____

Pack Up

It's time for summer vacation!

Which things will you pack?

Draw a line from the suitcase to each.

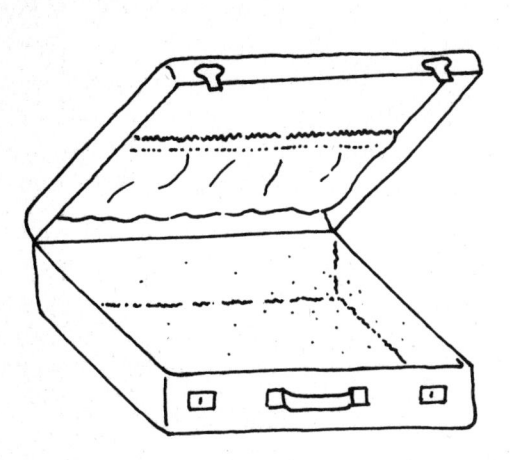

Write a story about where you are going.

_____
_____
_____
_____
_____
_____

Making Inferences   21   Everyone WRITE

Name _____

Riddle Faces

Finish the pictures.
Then choose one.
Write a story about it.

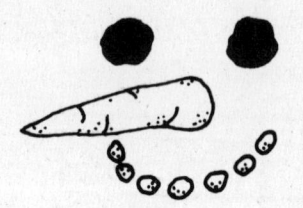

_____
_____
_____
_____
_____
_____

Part/Whole Relationships   22   Everyone WRITE

Name _____

Silly Signs

Read aloud the silly signs.
Then write one of your own.
Use words that begin in the same way.

Jan's Jumbo Jams

Sheila's Shiny Shoe Shop

Paula's Perfect Pumpkins

_____
_____
_____
_____
_____

Now read your sign aloud—FAST!

Classifying   23   Everyone WRITE

Name _____

Sand Castles

What will the beach look like tomorrow?
Write a story to tell why.

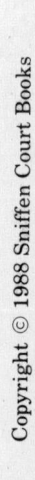

Anticipating Probabilities — Everyone WRITE

Name _____

A-maze-ing Trip

Draw a line through the maze to get to the tree house.
Start here.

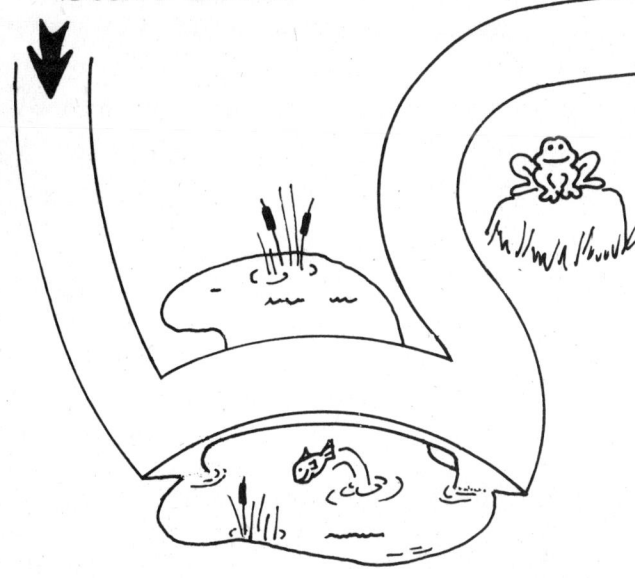

Write a story about your maze trip.
Tell in order what things you passed.

_____
_____
_____
_____
_____
_____

Sequencing 25 Everyone WRITE

Name _____

Haunted House

Close your eyes.

Put your finger on a number in the circle.

Move that many spaces on the path.

Write the words from the spaces you land on under the right heading on the next page.

Keep playing until you get to the house.

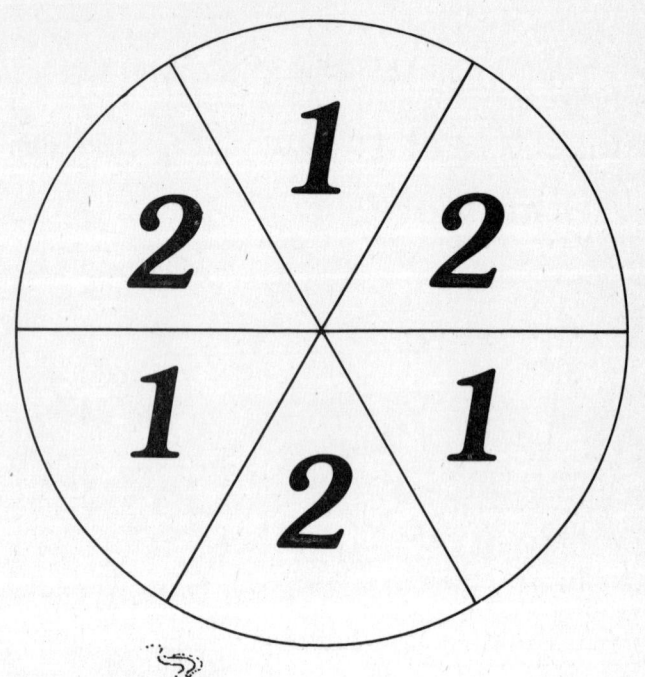

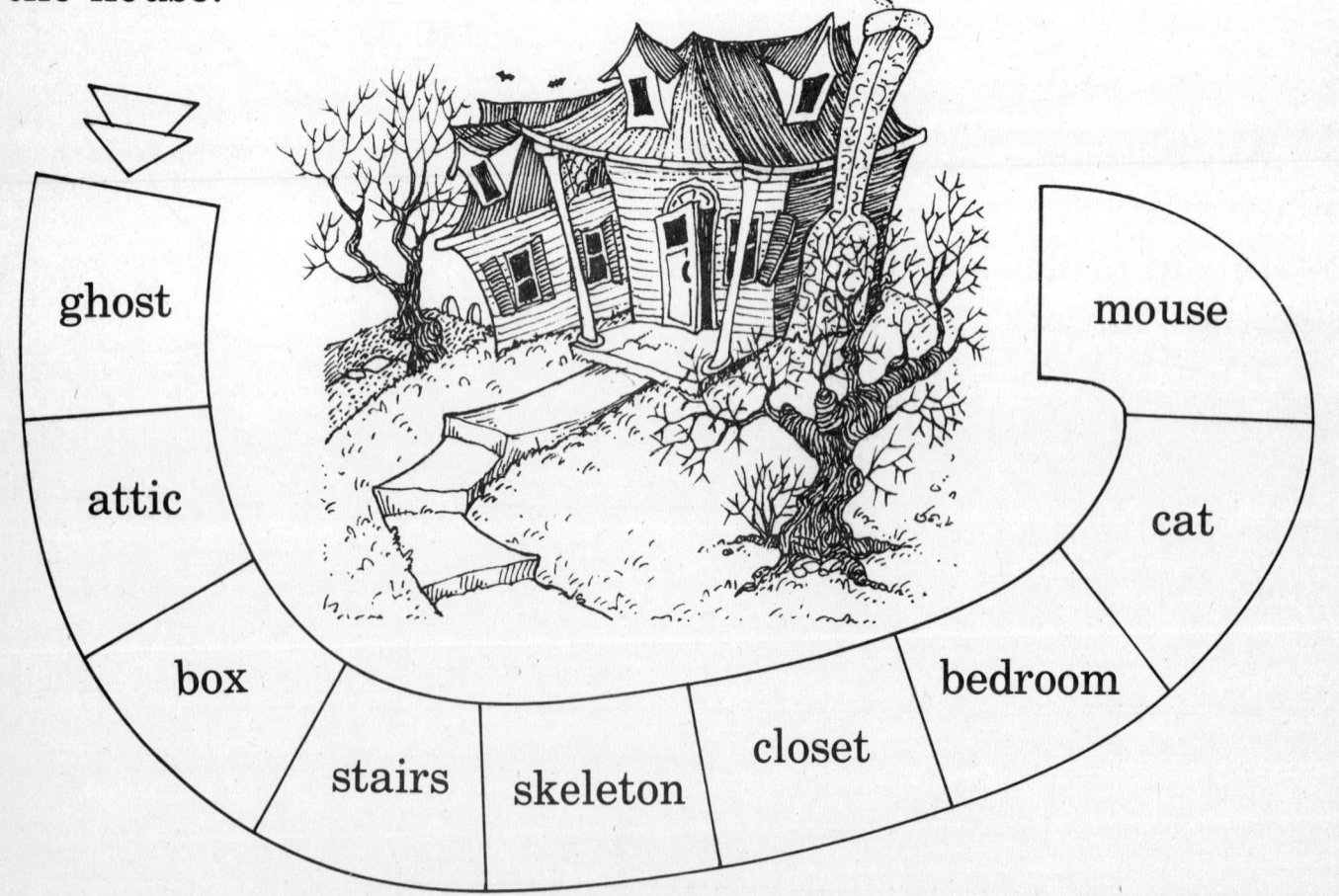

Path spaces: ghost, attic, box, stairs, skeleton, closet, bedroom, cat, mouse

Classifying — 26 — Everyone WRITE

Copyright © 1988 Sniffen Court Books

Name _____

Haunted House

WHO | WHERE

Write a story about the house.
Use the words you landed on.

Synthesizing　　27　　Everyone WRITE

Name _____

A Time Piece

Look at the time words.
A <u>year</u> is the longest time.
A <u>month</u> is the next longest.
Where do the other two words belong?
Write them in the correct boxes.

    year
    month
    week
    day

Choose the <u>shortest</u> time in the box.
Write a story about how you might spend it.

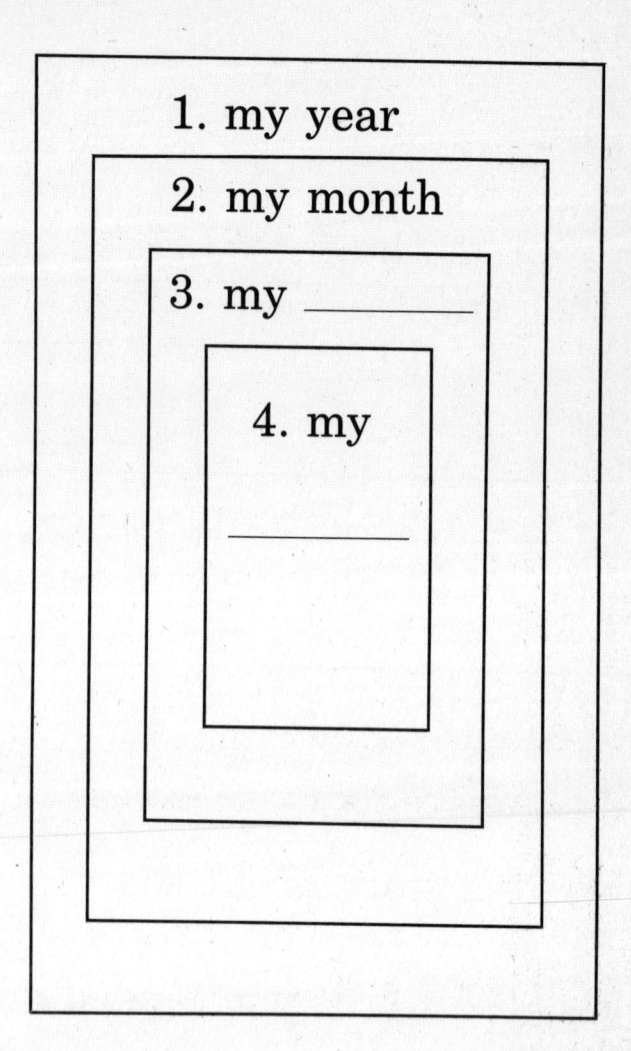

1. my year
2. my month
3. my _____
4. my _____

_____
_____
_____
_____
_____
_____

Part/Whole Relationships — Everyone WRITE

Name _____

What Happened?

Nan left these things in the sun.

It was <u>very</u> hot.

Color the things that stayed the same.

Circle the ones that didn't.

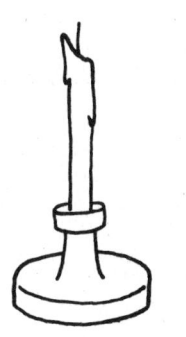

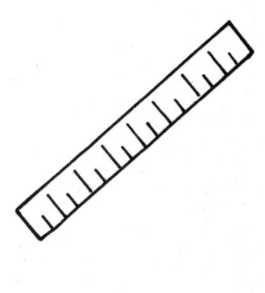

WORD BOX

| melt | candle | drip |
| cone | hot | soft |

Write a story to tell why some things changed.

Use the word box.

Developing Story Logic — Everyone WRITE

Name _____

The Green Cat Paws

Write a story in the spaces.

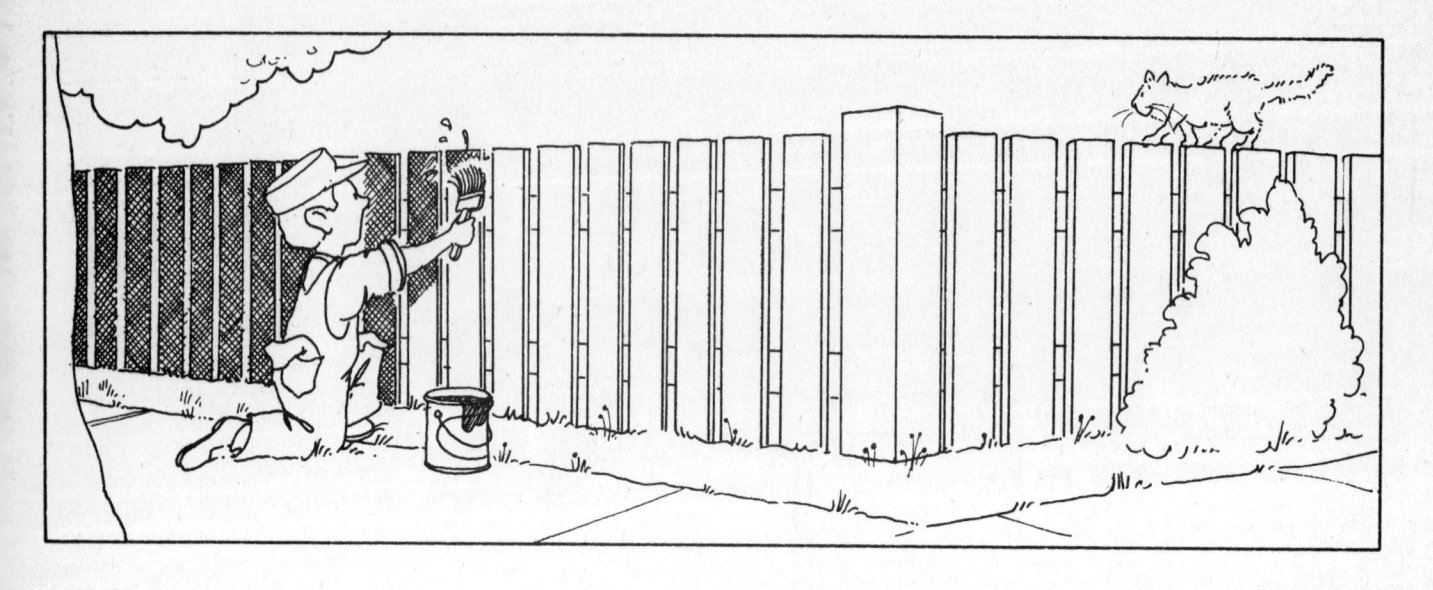

_____
_____

_____

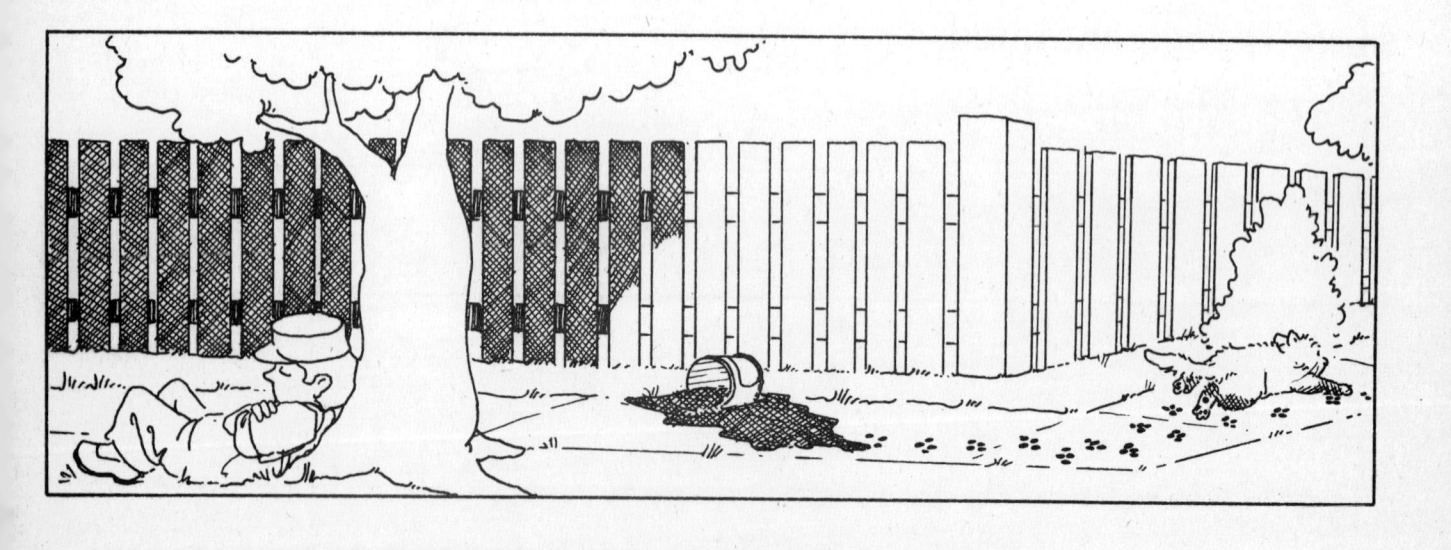

Making Inferences — Everyone WRITE

Name _____

The Green Cat Paws

What happens next?
Draw a picture and write
your ending.

_____

_____

_____

_____

_____

Predicting Outcomes — 31 — Everyone WRITE

Name _____

Who is Ed?

Cut and paste to finish the story.

Ed is very big.

He is an ☐ .

He has a long ☐ .

He has 2 large ☐ .

Ed also has great big ☐ .

Draw Ed in the box.
Tell one more thing about him.

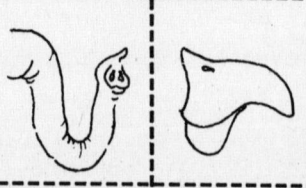

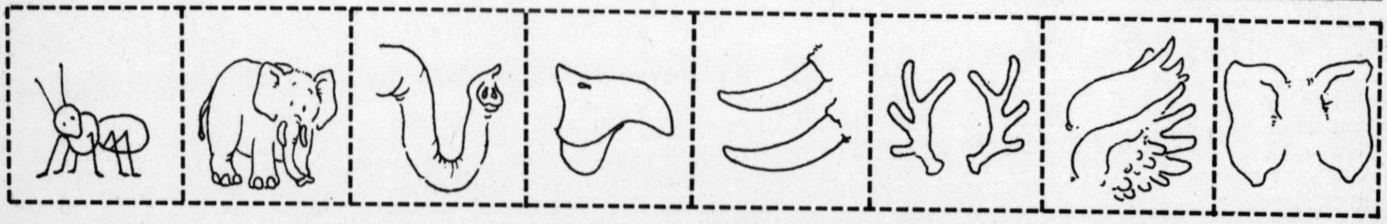

Making Inferences — 32 — Everyone WRITE

Name _____

Put Out the Fire

Jan is afraid.
The trash is on fire.
Who will put it out?
How?

Draw a picture.
Write the story.

Solving a Problem — 33 — Everyone WRITE

Name _____

Riding High

Neil wants to get up.
How can Ed help him?

Draw a picture.
Write the story.

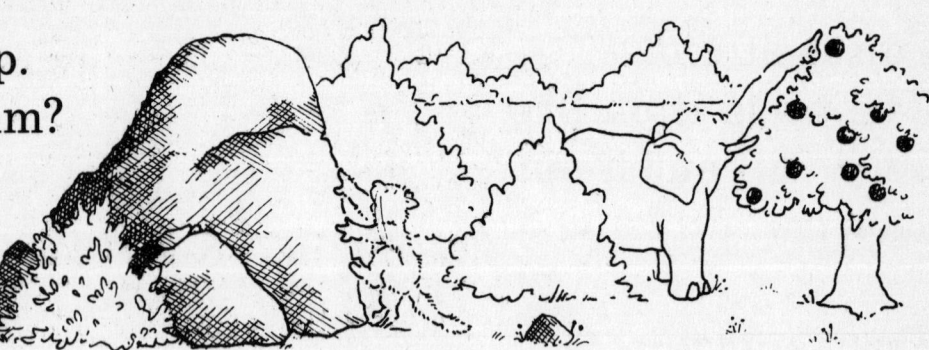

Solving a Problem — 34 — Everyone WRITE

Name _____

In the Mud

Whoops!
The car is stuck in the mud.
Mr. May can't get it out.
How can Ed help?

Draw a picture.
Write a story.

Solving a Problem — Everyone WRITE

Name _____

From Clue to Clue

Look at the pictures.
Write a sentence to tell about each one.

___

___

___

___

Sequencing　　　36　　　Everyone WRITE

Name _____

From Clue to Clue

How does the story end?
Write an ending.

_____

_____

_____

_____

_____

Draw a picture of your
ending.

Name _____

The Empty Cage

Uh-oh!
The bird is gone!
Draw the bird that lives in this cage.

Why did the bird go away?
Write a story.

_____
_____
_____
_____
_____

Building Hypotheses   38   Everyone WRITE

Name _____

Name the Place

Write a place to keep each thing.
Use the Word Bank.

WORD BANK
pocket   purse
bank   cabinet
dresser   closet

1.  _____
_____

2. 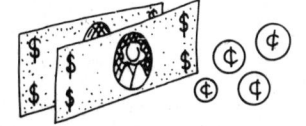 _____
_____

3.  _____
_____

Choose one thing from the list.
Think of a <u>different</u> place to keep it.
Write about it.

_____
_____
_____
_____

Proposing Alternatives — 39 — Everyone WRITE

Name _____

Just Pretend

Circle the pictures that show something real.

Color the pictures that show something make-believe.

Dogs like to read.

Children can skate.

Flowers can smile.

Rainbows make good slides.

Birds live in nests.

Real and Make Believe

Name _____

Just Pretend

Choose a make-believe picture.
Write a story about it.
Draw your own picture to go with the story.

_____
_____
_____
_____
_____

Real and Make Believe — Everyone WRITE

Name _____

Finding the Words

This bracelet is full of words! Some of the words are written here.

Add more words from the letters in <u>bracelet</u> to the list.

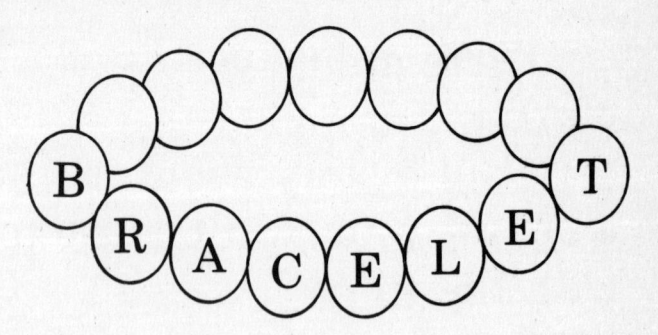

ate

cab

beet

Choose three of the words you wrote. Use them in a story.

Name _____

Can Code

There are three "cans" in this story. Can you find them?
(Hint: Name the word that each picture stands for.)
Then finish the story by adding your own pictures and words.
Use the words on the cans to help you.

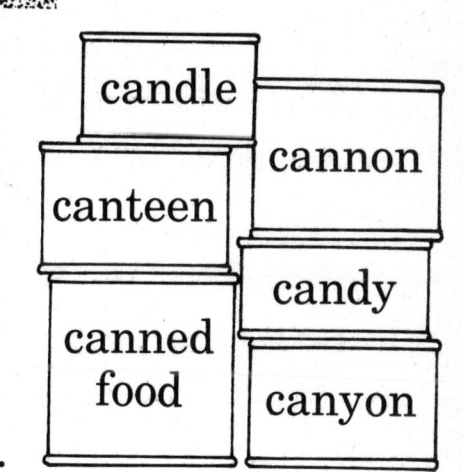

candle
cannon
canteen
candy
canned food
canyon

The twins packed the [canoe] for their trip.

Sandy put in some [cantaloupe] for lunch. Andy packed their pet [canary]. He also added a [_____] and [_____]. Then Sandy put in some [_____].

Then, _____

Recognizing Structure   43   Everyone WRITE

Name _____

Mirror Mary

Mary likes to do just what others do not.

If you go left, she goes right.

If you go in, she goes out.

Look at the picture.

What do you think Mary will do here?

Write what happens when she does it.

_____
_____
_____
_____
_____
_____

Anticipating Probabilities — 44 — Everyone WRITE

Name _____

Birthday Notes

Cut the page along the .... lines.

Fold the paper along the .... lines to make a card.

Write a silly rhyme on the outside of the card.

Draw a picture to go with your rhyme.

Inside, write a birthday note to a friend.

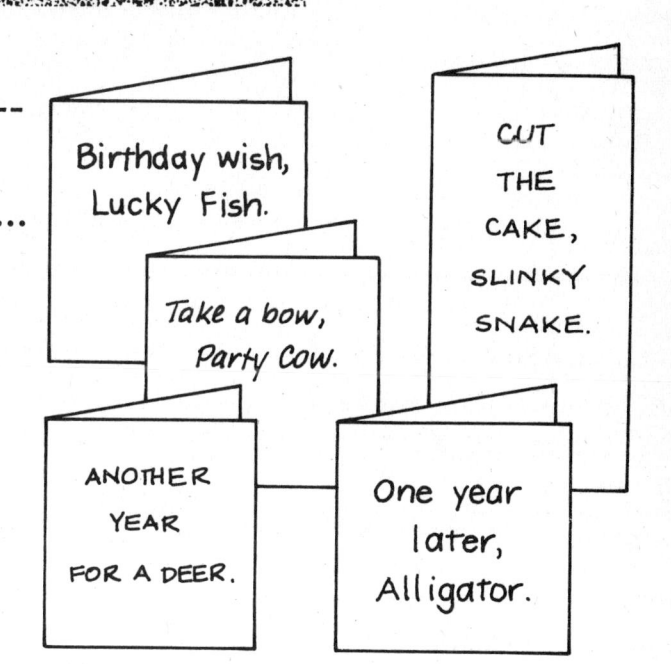

- Birthday wish, Lucky Fish.
- CUT THE CAKE, SLINKY SNAKE.
- Take a bow, Party Cow.
- ANOTHER YEAR FOR A DEER.
- One year later, Alligator.

Name _____

What's the Problem?

What is going on?
Write a story about the
problem of Ollie Octopus.

_____
_____
_____
_____
_____
_____

Identifying Problems — 46 — Everyone WRITE

Name _____

Talk Time

What did he say?

Then what did <u>he</u> say?

Write a story.
Tell what happened.

_____

_____

_____

_____

_____

_____

Drawing Conclusions — 47 — Everyone WRITE

Name _____

Island Hop

Close your eyes.

Put your finger on a number in the circle.

Move that many spaces on the path.

Write the words from the spaces you land on under the right heading on the next page.

Keep playing until you get to the island.

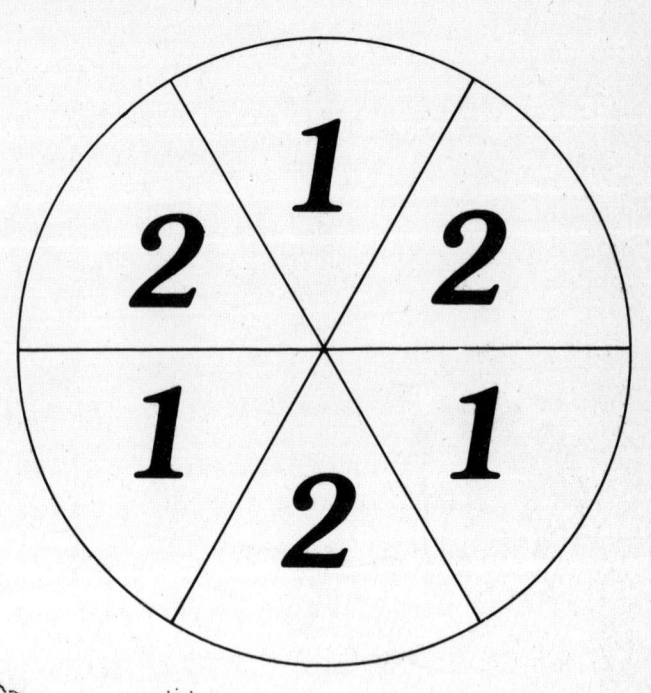

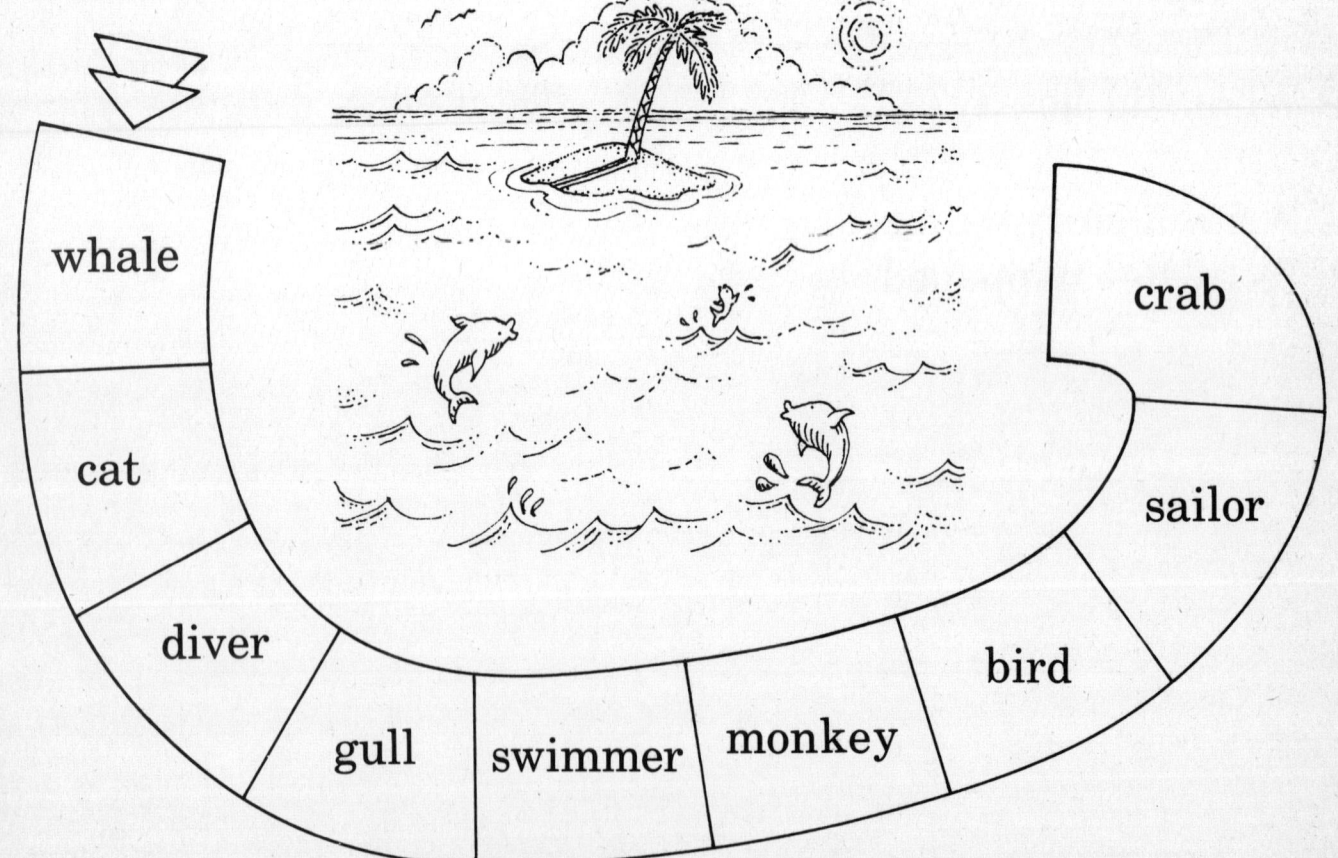

Path spaces: whale, cat, diver, gull, swimmer, monkey, bird, sailor, crab

Classifying — 48 — Everyone WRITE

Copyright © 1988 Sniffen Court Books

Name _____

Island Hop

ANIMALS	PEOPLE
_____	_____
_____	_____
_____	_____
_____	_____
_____	_____

Write a story about getting to the island.
Use the words you landed on.

_____
_____
_____
_____
_____

Synthesizing | 49 | Everyone WRITE

Name _____

Help Wanted

Study the pictures of Kirk and Sally.
What is wrong?
Choose one.
Write directions to tell Kirk or Sally what to do.

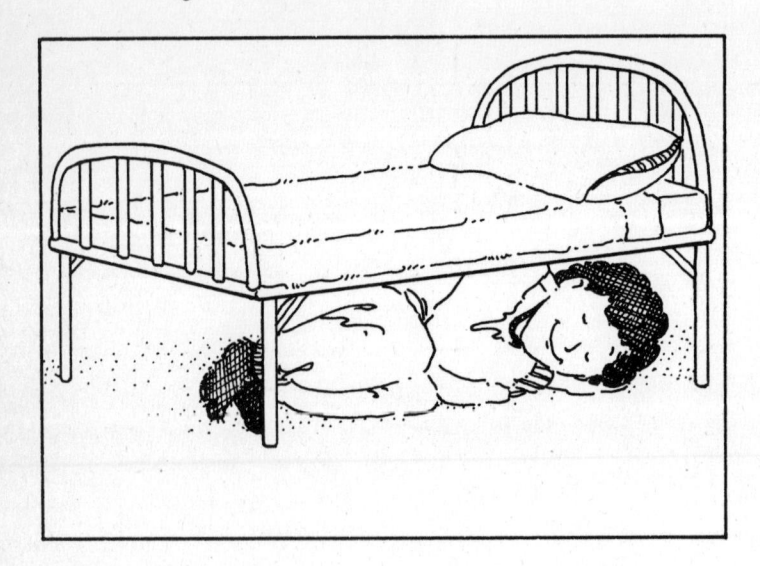

Help for Kirk or Sally

1. _____
_____

2. _____
_____

3. _____
_____

Using Sequence 50 Everyone WRITE

Name _____

V's Wheels

Finish the story about **V**.

Use your own pictures.

V got new 🛼 . She put them on and went **2**

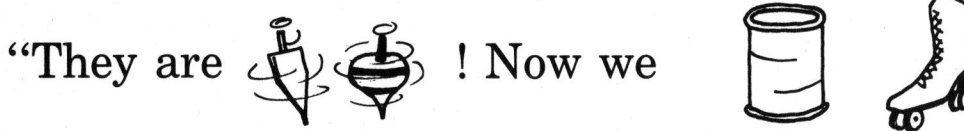

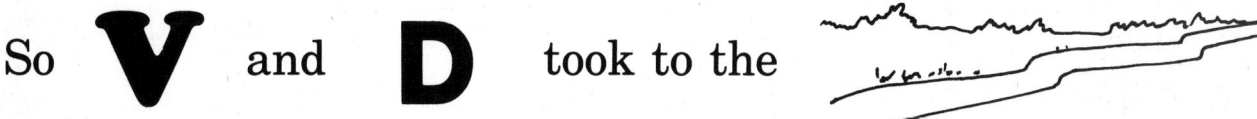

C her friend **D** . " **G** ," said **D** .

"They are 🎲🎲 ! Now we 🥫 🛼 together."

So **V** and **D** took to the 〰️〰️ .

They went down ☐ and they went over ☐ .

They met ☐ and they saw ☐ .

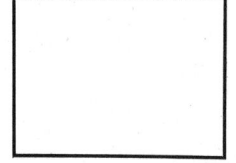

Then _____

_____

_____

_____

Name _____

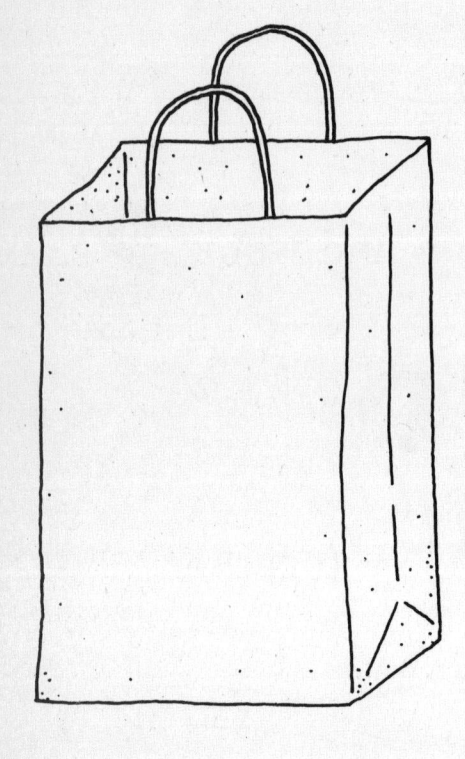

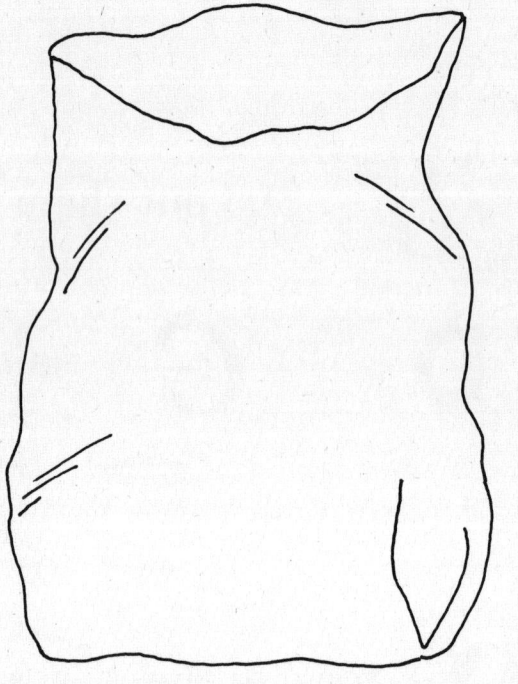

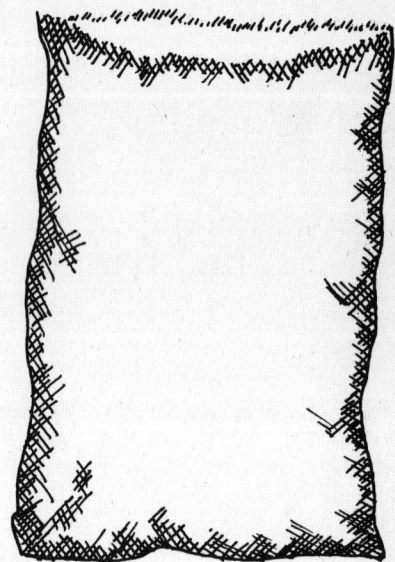

In the Bag

Draw what is in each bag.
Then choose one bag and
write a story about it.

_____
_____
_____
_____
_____
_____
_____

Building Hypotheses | 52 | Everyone WRITE

Name _____

The Silly Dream

Why is Ken smiling in his sleep?

Draw a picture to show.

Write a story about Ken's funny dream.

_____
_____
_____
_____
_____

Building Hypotheses — 53 — Everyone WRITE

Name _____

Cartoon Capers

What do the people in the cartoon say and think?
Fill in the spaces to tell.

■ Making Inferences ■ 54 ■ Everyone WRITE ■

Name _____

Cartoon Capers

_____
_____

Write your ending here.
_____
_____
_____
_____
_____
_____

Predicting Outcomes — 55 — Everyone WRITE

Copyright © 1988 Sniffen Court Books

Title Time

Read the story.
Then write a title and an ending for it.

_____

_____

Mark ran down the sidewalk.

He didn't want to be late for John's party.

John had said there would be a surprise.

Fast ... Fast ... Faster ran Mark.

OOps! He didn't see the big puddle.

Mark slipped and fell.

What a splash he made!

Sadly he got up and shook some water off.

He sure was wet.

What a way to go to a party.

Mark walked the rest of the way to John's house.

"Hi, Mark!" said John.
"I see you're already wet. How did you know I am having a swimming party? That's my surprise!"

Mark said, _____

_____

_____

Summarizing — 56 — Everyone WRITE

Name _____

Over the Hill

What is on the other side of the hill?

Write a story to tell about it.

_____
_____
_____
_____
_____
_____

Building Hypotheses   Everyone WRITE

Name _____

Valentine Message

Cut out the page along the .... lines.

Fold the paper along the .... lines to make a card.

Write a silly rhyme on the outside of the card.

Draw a picture to go with your rhyme.

Inside, write a Valentine wish for a friend.

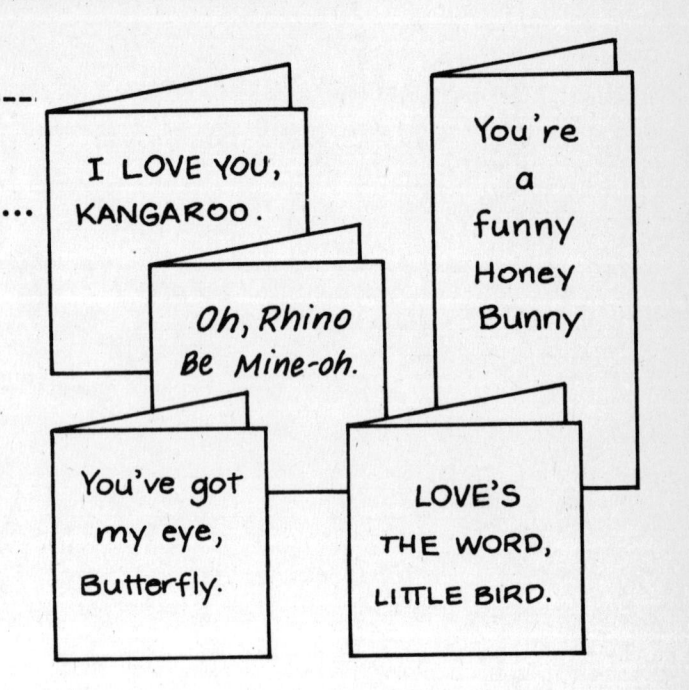

I LOVE YOU, KANGAROO.

You're a funny Honey Bunny

Oh, Rhino Be Mine-oh.

You've got my eye, Butterfly.

LOVE'S THE WORD, LITTLE BIRD.

Conducting a Project

Everyone WRITE

Name _____

Story in a Picture

Study the picture.
Circle five things that do not belong.
Then write a story about the things that _do_ belong.

_____
_____
_____
_____
_____
_____

Judging Relevance 　　　　59　　　　Everyone WRITE

Name _____

How Come?

Sometimes it is fun to tell make-believe stories about real things.

Choose one topic.

Write a make-believe story about how it came to be.

How did the wind get so strong?

Why are the seas salty?

Why are lemons sour?

Why do bunnies have long ears?

Why don't the stars talk?

_____
_____
_____
_____
_____

Proposing Alternatives

Name _____

Now What?

What happens next?
Write the story.

_____

_____

_____

_____

_____

_____

Predicting Outcomes — Everyone WRITE

Name _____

Partners and Pairs

Find something in the top row and something in the bottom row that are used for the same thing.

Draw a line to match each pair.

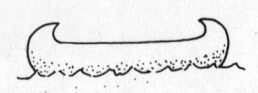

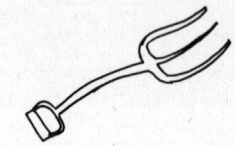

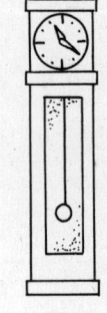

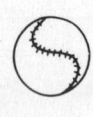

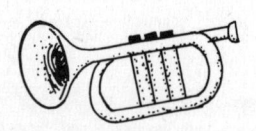

Choose one pair.
Tell how they are alike.
Tell how they are different.

_____
_____
_____
_____
_____
_____

Comparing and Contrasting — Everyone WRITE

Name _____

Opening Doors

Finish the pictures.
Draw a building to go with each door.

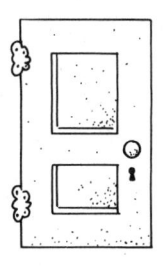

Choose one building and write a story about what's behind the door.

_____
_____
_____
_____
_____
_____

Part/Whole Relationships　　　63　　　Everyone WRITE

Name _____

A-maze-ing Ride

Draw a line through the maze to get to the wishing well.
Start here.

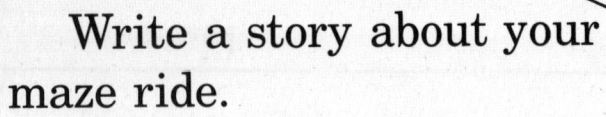

Write a story about your maze ride.
Tell in order what things you passed.

_____
_____
_____
_____
_____
_____

Sequencing